GETTING

By Rick Singer

with R.M. Hendershot

GAINING ADMISSION TO YOUR COLLEGE OF CHOICE

There is no passion to be found playing small –
in settling for a life that is less than the one you are
capable of living.

Nelson Mandela

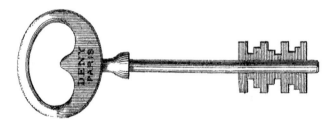

         ISBN 978-0-615-83797-0

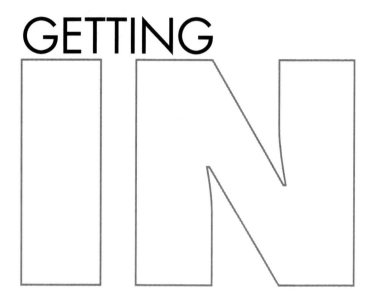

GETTING IN

PART I

BEFORE YOU BEGIN

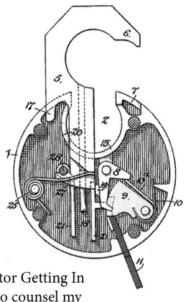

As a high school administrator Getting In taught me a ton about how to counsel my own students   – John Bryne

CHAPTER 1

GETTING INTO COLLEGE IS A SCIENCE, NOT AN ART

This book is full of secrets.

The college application process seems mysterious from the outside. Transcripts and essays, financial aid and letters of recommendation — somehow a small mountain of paper all boils down to a simple yes or no. You get in, or you don't. You succeed, or you fail. And no one knows why.

Actually ... I know why. And so do you.

I've been coaching students on the process for 26 years. I've run essay workshops from California to China and from South Carolina to Saudi Arabia. I've also read applications at universities all over the U.S. for domestic and international students, which means I'm one of the people who decides who gets in and who doesn't. I am a practitioner of that mysterious art. And I'll tell you a secret.

It's not an art. It's a science.

Colleges and universities have the process boiled down to numbers. Grades matter this much. Test scores matter that much. Activities matter a certain amount. Essays and letters of recommendation figure in a particular way. In this book, you'll find out exactly how much each element matters — and how to make it all work to your advantage.

Some of these secrets have been staring you in the face all along. A few will shock you. All will help you succeed, whether you're a straight-A overachiever or a struggling C-average.

The goal of this book is to help you find the right college, get in, and excel. And the first step in that process is turning the page.

Are you ready to learn the secrets?

CHAPTER 2

BRAND YOURSELF

Getting into college is a lot like selling iPads or cans of Coca-Cola. It's all about branding.

Whether you know it or not, whether you believe it or not, you have a personal brand. Anyone reading your application, your list of honors and activities, or your personal statement should be able to see in an instant who you are. Maybe you're the standout athlete, or the straight-A brainiac, or the virtuoso musician. Everything you do supports that image. Everything you do builds your brand. You win championships, blow the grading curve, pack the halls at your concerts. Everyone can see exactly who you are. The more you do, the clearer and stronger your brand becomes.

If you don't know what your personal brand is yet, it's time to name it and claim it. Because you need a strong brand.

The great thing about a strong brand is that any school that admits you knows exactly what it's getting — and knows that's something that it wants. You can order a Big Mac at any McDonald's on Earth and know exactly what you'll get. The trick is creating the Big Mac in the first place, and then convincing people that they want it.

Building your personal brand is all about finding and following your passion. Whatever you love, whatever you're good at, do it a lot and do it well. So start a business. Make a movie. Found a charity. Travel the world. Build something. Invent something. Change something. Do something! I can show you how, but ultimately it's your hard work that will open the door to the college of your choice. So don't wait. It's time to get going.

Your brand depends on you.

PART II
GET READY

Why should I do this and not do that...
I needed clear, comprehensive answers.
Getting In gave them to me.

– Jill Kaufman

CHAPTER 3

IT IS A JOURNEY

Your school has a plan for its students. You take certain classes, pass certain tests, jump through certain hoops, and go on to a certain destiny. Whether they tell you or not, your teachers, your principal, and your counselors have a plan for your life. They know how you can fulfill that plan, and they can help you make it.

And they can still be dead wrong.

Think of your school's plan like a road map. You follow a line across the landscape, passing through set points to get to a set destination — a certain college, a given career. But what if you don't want to go there? What if you're headed for somewhere else entirely?

You'll have to leave the road map.

Centuries ago, sailors navigating through strange waters used the stars to chart their course. They knew that landscapes change — mountains rise and fall, rivers shift course, cities crumble — but the stars don't. When you leave the map, you have to follow your star.

Look closely at your schedule of classes and your counselor's advice. Does your school's plan take you where you want to go? Does it teach you what you'll need to know in your future? Too often, high schools advise students and their families to take the classes that the school feels are appropriate, even when the students and families feel differently. Don't be afraid to question their reasoning! They might well be right about most students and wrong about you!

I've lost count of the number of times I've heard counselors say, "This is a good plan — it's how we've done things for years!" But the world is always changing; what worked years ago may not work now. And no two students are alike. If you feel you should be taking different classes, joining different activities, or charting a different course, don't let your school tell you that you can't. They have the road map, but you have the stars.

CHAPTER 4
BUILD A FOUNDATION OF CLASSES

Colleges are looking for certain classes. They want to see that you've studied the right subjects and done well in them. That means you have to take the right classes — and that starts in middle school.

You read that right. Middle school. As soon as you're allowed to choose your classes, you become responsible for your own education. Here's how to make the most of that.

The five core areas that colleges look at are math, English, science, social science, foreign languages, and the fine arts. So lock in your preparation in these areas. Take the most advanced math classes you can handle in middle school so you can get a jump on high-school math. Add a foreign-language elective if your school doesn't require it — French and Spanish are popular languages that you'll likely be able to continue studying in high school, but more schools each year are adding languages like Japanese, Chinese, and Korean, as well as languages like German and Latin that can give you a good foundation for learning other languages later.

Take the most advanced science classes you can, and take every opportunity to do experiments and/or work in a laboratory. It's good preparation for high-school science. You'll also want to read as much as you can, mixing classics with contemporary and "fun" books, to build your grasp of vocabulary and English mechanics for English classes. (Even comic books can help here, if you read the right comic books. It's the reading that matters!)

Finally, get involved in at least one fine art while you're in middle school: music, drama, visual arts, anything. It might become an essential piece of your personal brand.

CHAPTER 5

RIGOR: TAKE THE HARD COURSES

In order to be considered at a top-flight college, you have to take the most rigorous classes your high school offers. These colleges demand no less than four years of English, math, science, social science, and foreign-language classes. That means that in both middle school and high school, you have to hit the ground running. Take those core subjects every quarter, or every semester, of every year. Take at least 5 core courses each semester. Don't let these areas slide.

And as soon as a high-level class opens up — honors, Advanced Placement, or International Baccalaureate — you want to be in it. Those are the courses colleges are looking for. They're established brands. An A in history can mean anything. An A in AP European History and a 5 on the AP Euro exam tells a college exactly what it's getting in you. These are Big Mac courses. You want to take those hard classes, because they reinforce your brand.

A big part of taking the hard classes, however, is knowing your own abilities. If you know you can't handle a full load of honors classes, consider cutting back a little and focusing on the five core areas and the courses that best support your personal brand. If you know one more honors class is going to kill all your grades, it's time to throttle back. But you'll be surprised at how much you can handle. When in doubt, push just a little bit more. Try just a little harder. There's a lot of room in the red zone.

CHAPTER 6

EVERY GRADE COUNTS

When I sit down with families and students of any age, one of the first questions I hear is, "Do these grades count?"

The answer is: from ninth grade on, every grade counts.

Colleges look at your complete high-school transcripts, beginning in your freshman year. Think about it — when they're considering your application, they can't see most of your senior grades because those haven't been assigned yet. They want all the information on you that they can find to make sure you're right for their school. They want students who will excel, graduate on time, and come back to give them lots of alumni dollars. They only have so many slots and they have to choose wisely. If you had that job, would you look at only a few classes?

Of course not. You'd want to learn as much about each candidate as you could. That means that every grade counts, and all grades count equally, because it's all grist for the mill.

Your grades in college-prep courses count. Your grades in non-college-prep courses count — not as much, but they reflect on your effort and focus. Your freshman grades count. Your senior grades count — I can't emphasize this enough, as some schools will revoke your admission if your grades drop in your last semester of high school. There are a few schools that don't count grades from your freshman and senior years (such as the University of California system), but they're few and far between. As a rule, every grade counts.

So don't let your Spanish grade slip just so you can get an A-plus in AP Calculus. (In fact, the A-plus itself is a bad idea — I'll explain that in a few pages.) Don't let any grades slide. Make every grade count — because every grade counts.

CHAPTER 7

HARD CLASSES SHOW YOUR WORK ETHIC

If every grade counts, you should stack your class schedule with easy-A classes, right? After all, A's are better than B's, right?

Wrong! A hard B is better than an easy A.

Colleges don't just look at your grades. They look at the classes you took to get those grades. It's all about academic rigor. Most colleges look at your honors or weighted GPA (the one that bumps honors and AP grades up a point), and give the advantage to students taking more rigorous courses. They assume that students who take honors or AP classes are more serious than those taking regular college-prep classes. If you're taking more challenging courses, you are showing passion for learning — and passion is the basis of the strongest brands. Colleges want students who take to learning with gusto. Nothing says gusto like a full slate of honors, AP, or IB courses.

So if you have a choice between earning a B in AP English Literature and earning an A in regular English, and you know you have the ability to achieve, take the AP option. That B in Advanced Placement is worth the same number of points on your GPA as the ordinary A, and the magic letters "AP" will move you closer to the head of the line.

CHAPTER 8
SUMMERS ARE A TIME TO BUILD YOUR BRAND

What you do with your summers should build your brand.

Summer school is a great option if you want to take some of the load off your school-year class schedule. It's also a good time to take basic courses so you have more room in your fall schedule for more rigorous ones. However, summer classes usually aren't as in-depth as year-long courses, nor are they offered without a price. There are two ways to get into summer school: fail a class (or get a D) or pay the school a significant fee. If you want to work in the sciences and you're thinking about taking biology, chemistry, or physics during the summer, think again. You'll learn more during the school year, and you'll be better prepared for college coursework and subject tests (more on those later). On the other hand, if taking a summer health class will let you tackle a more rigorous science class in the fall, go for it!

There are other great ways to build your brand during the summer, too. Take courses at a local community or four-year college. Work a summer job, volunteer, or intern in a field where you hope to work. Join in brand-building extracurricular activities — athletics, fine arts, research, leadership. Build a robot in your garage. Make a film with your friends. Help out at a soup kitchen or shadow a hospital doctor. Whatever your brand is, your summers should support it.

CHAPTER 9

TAKE COLLEGE COURSES WHILE YOU'RE IN HIGH SCHOOL

Nothing gets a college's attention like a high-school student who's already been to college. And nothing builds your résumé like using a local four-year or community college to fill the gaps in your high school's offerings.

Between budget cuts, scheduling conflicts, and a one-size-fits-all attitude, your high school may not be able to offer you the advanced classes you need in math, science, English, and foreign languages. Community colleges in particular are great at offering these core subjects at a very reasonable cost. A shocking number of college students arrive at school totally unprepared in the five core areas, and so community colleges make a point of offering basic college courses that do the job of the advanced high-school courses those students missed. From there, it's a short leap to higher-level courses that look great on an application.

Many college systems also have articulation agreements with each other — special deals that let students take their credits from one school and apply them to a degree at another. Look at those agreements. The more credits you have as an incoming college freshman, the better-prepared you'll be to jump right into the classes you really want.

College coursework in high school has other advantages, too. You'll learn to navigate a college's registration system, find your way around a strange campus, and deal with college students and professors on a social level. Passing college-level courses while you're in high school tells your college of choice that you've already mastered these life skills as well as the class curriculum.

GETTING IN: WHITNEY

Whitney was a great kid — 3.0 GPA, heavily involved in social activities, and probably the most popular kid in her high school. Everybody loved her. You couldn't not love Whitney — it would be like hating sunshine, or kittens.

There was just one problem. Whitney had a learning disability. And it wasn't diagnosed until tenth grade.

She was a fighter, but she was at a disadvantage. She studied four or five hours per night and sweated blood over every homework assignment ... and she failed every test from tenth grade on. It didn't matter how much she prepared, or how well she thought she'd do. She made B's in her classes only because of her homework, and everyone told her a four-year college was out of reach.

Until tenth grade, she'd always been able to get by — speaking in class, doing hands-on activities that appealed to her tactile and auditory learning styles. After the diagnosis, though, she had to get serious. After months of wrangling, she found ways to take tests orally and physically — answering verbal questions from teachers, demonstrating math problems on the board. Her test scores doubled overnight.

Whitney still wanted to attend a four-year college, but was told she'd never make it with her limitations. She got extra time on the SAT, but no auditory help, so her scores were low, and she was convinced she was headed for community college.

But with my help, Whitney and her parents began looking into schools with disability programs. Some of them were what you might call bronze medalists; they had bare-bones aids, just what the law requires and nothing else. The silver medalists had more engaging programs, but still required students to seek out all the help themselves. We wanted Whitney at a gold-medal school — one that would check in with students and stay on top of their progress. And after Whitney wrote a strong application essay, she got plenty of acceptances — the University of Oregon, Amherst, and plenty more. We finally settled on the University of Arizona, which was glad to give her oral exams and extra time on tests.

She graduated in four years and now has a stellar career in public relations. Not bad for a disadvantaged fighter.

CHAPTER 10
GET A TUTOR!

Once there were no teachers — only tutors.

Tutor is the Latin word for teacher. For hundreds of years, the lucky few students who got an education got it from tutors — well-educated men, and occasionally women, who worked with students one-on-one and in small groups to teach them what they needed to know to succeed. It was customized education at its finest, before big schools were invented.

These days, of course, everyone knows that only struggling students need tutors. Everyone knows that tutors are only there to help you when you're flunking math or failing history. Everyone knows that good students don't need help.

And everyone is wrong.

The competition to get into the best colleges is fierce. Smart students take every advantage they can get. They work with their teachers after school, set up study groups, and yes, hire tutors. They don't risk having a bad day on a test or an assignment. They seek help first — the help everyone says they don't need.

A good study group or the right tutor can teach you exactly what you need to know, when you need to know it. That help can mean the difference between an A and a B, between honors and remedial, between acceptance and rejection. It's another arrow in your quiver; don't toss it out just because of what everyone says.

Everyone's not going to college. You are.

CHAPTER 11
AIM FOR EXCELLENCE

There's an old saying in my family: "We're not raising chickens for Colonel Sanders; we're raising eagles to fly." The idea is that you're supposed to grow up to soar on your own, not flap around in the dirt like a chicken. Everything you do should be focused on the goal of flight.

But what do you do if your GPA makes you look like an old hen?

If you aren't taking honors courses, or your grades are low, it's not too late. Colleges and universities are looking for students that improve during high school. Even if your freshman and sophomore records stink, you can always turn things around. Often, four-year schools will offer conditional admittance to improving students as long as those students continue to achieve during their eighth and final semester.

Did you know that every high-school freshman starts out ranked first in his or her class? It's true. On day one, everybody is #1. Then some students' grades plummet, assignments go missing, and test scores sink. But if you've ever watched an eagle taking off, you know that the bird might start off with a downward swoop, and soon he'll soar skyward. So pull up.

If your grades are sinking, study harder. Hit the library. Get a tutor. Suck up to your teachers — they'll tell you what to do to turn a B-plus (or even a C-plus) into an A-minus. There's always hope if you're willing to work hard and do the right thing. It's never too late.

On the ground, even an eagle can look like a chicken. It's what happens in the sky that counts.

CHAPTER 12

GO FOR THE MINUS, NOT THE PLUS

You should never get a B-plus.

Plus grades are a waste of effort. A B-plus is worth exactly three points to your grade point average. So is a B. So is a B-minus. So what's the point in getting a B-plus?

More importantly, what's the point in getting a B-plus when you could have an A-minus?

Think about the last time you got a plus grade — B-plus, C-plus, even D-plus. What did you tell your parents? Did it sound something like, "I was so close"? Maybe you even pinched the air to show how close you were. You were this close!

So what's stopping you from doing this much more?

For most students, grades will be the single most important factor in the college admissions process. Colleges and universities don't weigh pluses and minuses. An A-minus is as good as an A-plus to them. So whenever possible, turn your C-pluses into B-minuses and your B-pluses into A-minuses.

That means working your teachers. Make yourself stand out. Talk to them before and after class, and listen to everything they say. Be useful around the classroom. Raise your hand. Go the extra mile — or at least the extra inch—on homework and tests. Ask to earn extra credit. Your teachers will tell you how to turn that plus into a minus, and if you're right on the edge and they like you, they might even slip you that last point you need.

Once you've got the minus, move on to the next class with a plus. You've got more minuses to earn.

CHAPTER 13

OPTIMIZE YOUR TALENTS

In middle school, try everything. In high school, do your best thing.

As early as possible, you want to join any extracurricular activity that looks interesting — athletics, performing arts, school activities, church/synagogue/civic organizations, leadership you name it. Middle school is the time to try everything and find out what you like best. Once you know your own interests, you can choose the best activities for high school. You can begin building your brand.

Once you're in high school, everything you do should support that brand. If you're an athlete, join a traveling team to build your skills and make the varsity squad. If you're in student government, run for class president (or any other office you can win). If you're in orchestra, try out for the youth symphony and work to become first chair. If you're in the school play, audition for the leading role and get involved in community theatre. Stay committed to whatever you've chosen, semester after semester and year after year. That consistent involvement will show up on your application, and make your brand clear to anyone reading it.

Extracurricular activities are your chance to stand out. Everyone has grades, and a lot of your competition has good grades — but you have your brand, inside and outside of class. You have to play to your strengths, so whatever interests you, get involved and stay involved.

CHAPTER 14

PASSION SHOWS

Have you ever heard someone tell you that the way to get into college was to keep up with your piano lessons? Play the violin even though you hate it? Play a popular sport just because it's popular?

Guess what? That someone was lying.

Colleges aren't looking for concert violinists — at least, not miserable ones. They're not looking for star football players who secretly hate football. Most colleges would rather admit a fanatical tiddlywinks player who loves tiddlywinks than let in a hundred tennis champions who don't actually like tennis. If you're pursuing an activity just because your parents tell you to, or because you think it looks good on an application, stop right now before somebody gets hurt.

Instead, follow your passion.

Find what you love, whether it's tennis or tiddlywinks. Write poetry. Raise chickens. Be a mime if you have to! Even if you have to start at Mime Level One, even if you'll never win the World's Greatest Mime award, even if your friends laugh at you when you get trapped in an invisible box, find your passion and follow it. Passion shows. Passion can't be faked. And passion is what colleges want.

Every college on Earth is looking for bright, passionate students who will make an impact on campus and in the community. They're looking for students who aren't afraid to do what they love and who will have fun doing it — because that means they'll keep doing it. <u>Persistence is a virtue, and passion is the driver of persistence. Follow your passion, and it will show on your application.</u>

And who knows? You might just turn out to be the world's greatest mime after all ...

CHAPTER 15
TWO TO THREE ATTRIBUTES, NOT TEN

Admissions officers aren't stupid. They know what it looks like when you join twenty-two different campus clubs just so you can list them on an application. They know that half of those clubs probably meet at the same time.

If you're playing on three sports teams and playing a messenger in the school play and volunteering at a soup kitchen and acting as assistant under-secretary to the treasurer of four different clubs, you're not fooling anybody. Colleges know you're padding your application, and they don't like it.

So instead of filling your activities list with a hundred things you don't actually do, choose the two to four things you care about most — and do them more. Love drama? Try out for a leading role instead of Third Spear Carrier. Love music? Practice until you make first chair in the orchestra, or start a band in your garage. Love soccer? Play for your school's team during the season and play club soccer the rest of the time. Take on a leadership role in your church youth group, or a charity, or a club. Being president of the Gerbil Appreciation Society counts for a more than standing in the background of a dozen club photos — especially since nobody starts a Gerbil Appreciation Society unless he/she loves gerbils.

A group of science-loving kids I know created a science academy for underserved middle-school students. Another group took Al Gore's slideshow from An Inconvenient Truth and started their own anti-global-warming campaign (amusingly called Inconvenient Youth).

Do what you love and do it a lot. Colleges will notice, and admissions officers will smile.

CHAPTER 16

KEEP TRACK OF ALL ACTIVITIES

An activity log is the cure for the dreaded application brain fart.

When you sit down to fill out your college applications, are you going to remember every detail of your time as a library assistant in ninth grade? Probably not. But if you want to come across as a bright, passionate student involved in your community, you'll want the ability to list the number of hours you spent shelving books. And that is why you keep an activity log.

Beginning in ninth grade (or whenever you're reading this), keep a written list of all your activities. Write down what role you play, what honors or awards you receive, how many hours you work per week or per month or per year. Keep the tally on your computer, or on a sheet of paper in a safe place, and update it regularly. Don't assume you can sit down once a month and remember everything; add information whenever you reasonably can. Say what you did, when and where you did it, and what happened as a result. Type or write neatly; don't trust your everyday handwriting.

It seems tedious now, but you'll be grateful for that tally sheet when you're typing away on your personal statement at two in the morning and you suddenly can't remember a single interesting thing you did in high school. You're never more than one brain fart away from sounding like you spent four years in a coma. So write it all down!

CHAPTER 17

FIND WAYS TO BE A LEADER

Whenever possible, be a leader in your passion.

Ideally, your core activities should center around your strongest interests. You spend a lot of time thinking about your favorite sport, or student government, or the A-V club. Why not put all that skullsweat to good use? It looks great on an application, it broadens your range of experiences, and most importantly, it teaches you skills you didn't even realize you'll need for college and beyond.

If you're shy, being club secretary will encourage you to talk to members, which will come in handy when you have to introduce yourself to your roommate in the freshman dorm. If you're a loner by nature, being captain of your lacrosse team will help sharpen those teamwork skills — and you'll be glad of it when a college professor assigns you to a group project. If you only have the time or energy for one or two activities, holding a leadership position in one of them will show everyone that you throw yourself into the things you love — and that tells colleges that you won't just sit silently in the back row of your classes for four years.

When in doubt, lead.

CHAPTER 18
TAKE A GOOD LOOK AT YOURSELF

Psst. Lean in close. I'm going to tell you a dirty secret of college admissions.

We don't care that much about your SAT scores.

The College Board wants you to think that your SAT scores are the single most important factor in college admissions. They want you to think you should take the SAT as many times as possible, straining to raise that precious score by even a few points. But while a perfect score is always impressive, and a high score is great, you've only got so many hours in the day. And if you have to choose between cramming for another SAT and studying for tomorrow's calculus test, go with the calculus.

You see, we admissions people care more about your rigorous curriculum, your personal brand, and your class rank than your SAT scores. We all know schools are giving out scholarships for high scores — buying numbers to raise their rankings. Scores everywhere are higher than they were in the past, too, because there are so many more opportunities to prepare for the test. That makes any SAT score, high or low, a lot less valuable.

And it's much easier to raise your GPA than it is to raise your SAT.

It's a lot simpler to go from a 3.6 grade point average to a 3.9 grade point average than it is to raise your ACT or SAT-1 scores from 29 to 34 or from 1200 to 1400. The difference in moving your grade point average might be as small as turning a couple of B-pluses into A-minuses. A few extra right answers on that calculus test could turn three grade points into four. And colleges will pay more attention to that GPA because it represents work you did day in, day out, for years, rather than three and a half hours of high-pressure answer-bubbling.

So put down 1000 SAT Vocabulary Words and pick up your math book. It'll pay off.

CHAPTER 19

CHECKMATE THE TEST

Even if you've never played chess, you've seen movies and television shows where somebody taps a piece down on a chessboard and proclaims, "Checkmate!" Across the board, another character groans or complains or tries to argue, but "checkmate" means the game is over.

Well, actually, it doesn't.

In chess, "checkmate" means that one player's king is out of legal moves and has no way to avoid being captured by the other player's piece. It means, "Everyone acknowledges the game is over, so why make things ugly?"

This is exactly what you have to do to the SAT and the ACT.

The SAT is designed to be stupid. It's a reasoning test, a game to learn how to answer questions. The ACT is about your knowledge and your academic foundation. Either way, if you've paid attention in school — if you've built up a good vocabulary, learned how to gather information from what you read, mastered the basics of English grammar, kept up with math, and practiced writing five-paragraph essays — you should have no problem getting a decent score on any test. If you haven't done one or more of those things, there are plenty of prep books and tutors out there, and I heartily recommend that you use them. With their help, these tests are easily beaten.

The SAT and ACT are wide open to you if you know how to plan. So read the books. Study with a tutor. Take practice tests. Write essays under a time limit. Learn new vocabulary words. Review grammar. Read whenever you get the chance. Pay attention in math class. Do your homework. Be smart; remember that these tests are stupid, and smart beats stupid.

The king of standardized tests is defenseless. Checkmate.

GETTING IN: GABE

Gabe was a good student. He had a 3.5 GPA and scored 1760 on his PSAT. But his parents were sure he could do better on the SAT. For a year, Gabe's parents made him take practice SATs — one section per day, five days a week, about 25 minutes per day, and a full practice test every weekend.

He hated it. I'm not going to lie — he loathed those tests.

Gabe had to make a flashcard for every word he didn't know — in a question, in a critical reading passage, anywhere. If he missed a math problem, he put it on a card, drawing the geometric figures if necessary. At the end of that year, he had about 200 math cards and 200 vocabulary cards. He ran through his vocabulary cards for ten minutes at breakfast and dinner, and his math cards at lunch and at bedtime. His mother quizzed him, too, and texted his father with his scores. Twenty to twenty-five cards per day, every day. Imagine the shouting matches!

A month before the SAT, his father gave him a full-length practice exam … and Gabe missed exactly two questions. His dad was sure his son had cheated, so he gave him the test again, this time sitting in the room to watch him.

This time, Gabe got a perfect score.

"It doesn't matter what you do to me," Gabe told his father. "You and Mom have been jerks to me, but I can take this test until the cows come home, and I won't need to cheat."

He took the real SAT a month later, and got a perfect score. Of course, he never wants to see an index card again …

PART III:
CHOOSE YOUR SCHOOL

Our confusion led to conflicts between my
husband, the kids and myself. Getting In
let us all know what was needed to get
accepted and allow the family to return
to "normal."   – Lani Lapidus

CHAPTER 20
ASK YOURSELF QUESTIONS

Two thousand years ago, anyone who wanted the answer to an important question went to the temple of Apollo at Delphi. Kings and paupers alike came to ask their questions of a priestess who was said to speak directly for Apollo, the Greek god of prophecy. But the prophecies were often vague or confusing. People misinterpreted them with catastrophic results. That's why to get into the temple, before consulting the god, every visitor had to walk past a two-word inscription in stone: "Know thyself."

Like all important decisions, choosing the right college depends on how well you know yourself. And you have to know before you ask an oracle, or anyone else, for their input.

There are a lot of factors to consider when you're deciding which college is right for you (and remember it's for you, not your parents or your friends or anyone else who won't be going there), but they all begin with knowing yourself. That means you have to ask yourself a few questions before you begin your search. None of these questions have right or wrong answers, but they're all answers you need to know:

— What values are most important to you?

— What are your personal strengths and qualities of character?

— What type of person would you like to become?

— Are you already thinking of a definite profession or career? If so, which one?

— What are the first words that come to mind when asked to describe yourself?

— What kind of academic record do you have?

— Do you work to your potential, or beyond or below your abilities?

— How much structure do you need? Are you able to work independently?

— What might be a possible major or concentration for you in college?

— What kind of learning environment do you thrive in?

— How independent, resourceful, creative, and motivated are you? (It's okay to say "not very," so be honest!)

— Why are you going to college?

— How well do you get along with your peers, faculty, and other adults?

— How do you react to pressure, challenge, or competition?

— What types of activities do you most enjoy? Do you want to pursue these in college?

— Do you have special hobbies and talents that require a special location, a special kind of program, or certain weather?

— If you had to choose a geographic location in which to go to school, which location would it be? (Pick at least two — you might be surprised at the results.)

— Do you want a school in an urban, residential, college-town or rural region? (Again, pick at least two.)

— What class size suits you best? Small (10 to 30)? Medium (50 to 200)? Large (200-plus)?

— What is your personal brand, and how do you create, or enhance it?

Answer these questions, and the oracle's answer will be a lot clearer.

CHAPTER 21
DO YOUR COLLEGE HOMEWORK

The more you know about the colleges you're considering, the more informed your decision will be. Just about any college will send you information — glossy brochures, course catalogs, DVDs. But first you need a list of schools to request information from. You need resources.

Your local bookstore should have at least a few college guides that fall into two categories: comparative and subjective. Comparative guides, considered the most objective sources, include books like Barron's, Peterson's, and the College Admission Handbook. They present only the facts and statistics about a college. Subjective guides, on the other hand, try to give you a feel for each institution and the students who attend it. They express an opinion, either one person's or a whole group's. These guides include those by Fiske, Princeton Review, and the Yale Daily News. Rugg's and Gourman guides rank programs within schools. Check with your school counselor or your school dean's office for these guides, and if all else fails, hit the library.

There are also hundreds of websites offering everything from advice on financial aid to virtual campus tours. Sites like CampusTours.com and CollegeView.com can be a big help, as can the websites of the Department of Education, FAFSA, and Sallie Mae. Check out the websites of your state's public college and university systems too. If you're interested in athletics, the NCAA website is a great place to start. Finally, there are websites catering to students looking at special-interest schools, such as historically black colleges and universities, Jewish schools, Jesuit and other Catholic schools, music conservatories, and schools for the visual and performing arts.

Don't be afraid to start out with a long list of possible schools. There will be plenty of ways to narrow it down later.

CHAPTER 22
PAYING FOR COLLEGE

Once you have your criteria worked out, you can set an application schedule. Take that list of schools and find out what you need to turn in and when. When are your application deadlines? What about early decision and/or early admission? Do you need to take any special tests or schedule an interview?

And never forget ... what are you going to do about money?

If you're not a trust-fund baby, don't panic. Most colleges and universities offer financial or merit aid of some kind, but you'll have to jump through some hoops for it. First and most importantly, know that financial-aid deadlines are different from application deadlines, and the paperwork is different. You may have to verify your household's income and your grades to show that you qualify for aid. Attend financial-aid workshops if you can to determine what kind of aid you need, what kind of aid you can get, and what you have to do to get it. Different schools have different systems and different responses to different levels of financial need. There are also specialty scholarships out there — private funding for everything from humorists to left-handed students to people named Zolp.

You may want to ask the schools you're considering if they're "need blind" in admissions. That means that an applicant's financial need plays no role in the admission decision. Colleges are generally willing to describe their policies in this area, so don't be afraid to ask. And because colleges are a business, even the need-blind ones want as many full-paying customers as possible — so some of them will offer you a small scholarship, without provocation, just to get you to come. You may be able to combine that scholarship with private aid and grants, too. The more you know, the stronger your financial game plan will be.

CHAPTER 23
VISIT SCHOOLS

When you're seriously considering a college, it's best to visit the campus and get a sense of the place. You will be tempted to schedule your campus tour when it's most convenient — during breaks like summer vacation.

Don't settle for that.

The best time to visit a college campus is when classes are in session. If you go to this school, most of your time there will be spent during the semester; don't you want to know what the place will be like then? You want to see the hustle and bustle of the college as it really is. Sure, the buildings and facilities are important, and those don't go anywhere over the summer, but the heart and soul of any school is its students. The people you'll sit next to in class, the people you'll be living with in the dorms and in college housing can make or break your college experience. You want to talk to them, ask them questions and get to know them before you make your decision. And the best time for that is while class is in session.

Of course, off-season tours are much easier to arrange, and they have their advantages too. The summer months allow you to take a more leisurely look at a school, touring at your own pace and going off the beaten path where necessary. I had a student once who couldn't be happy with a school until she'd sat in an empty classroom and listened to the silence; that's hard to do during the regular semester.

But if you find a school you like during the summer, return in the fall. There's no substitute for seeing education in its natural habitat — especially when that habitat might soon be yours.

CHAPTER 24

LOOK FOR THE TEAM YOU CAN BEAT

If varsity athletics are a part of your college search, plan your campus tours accordingly. Contact the coaches at schools you'll be visiting well in advance, and let them know you're coming. Provide an unofficial transcript and test scores if you can. Ask whether you can set up a meeting with the coach during your visit and try to arrange an opportunity to look at the athletic facilities and watch a team practice or game. You can learn more from watching an hour of play than you can from a hundred brochures. Remember that every coach is "hired to be fired" — he knows that as his teams get better and better, expectations will rise, and he'll be sacked as soon as he fails to meet those new expectations. So watch for that cycle, take advantage of it, and don't take coaches too seriously.

Whenever you visit a school, jot down your impressions of the campus, the facilities, and the athletic programs. Does this school make athletics a priority? Is your sport well-funded? Does the student body support athletes? Do the coaches and players seem like people you'd want to spend time with? Can you see yourself there?

One more tip — if you watch a practice or a game and think you can make the team, then you're out of luck. You won't get recruited or get any help getting in, unless you're better than the team. If you can be the top player on day one, the coach will bend over backwards to recruit you. Look for the team where that can happen.

Perhaps the hardest part of touring a college with a focus on athletics is remembering that athletics can't be your only focus. You're not going to college just to play a sport — you're going for an education. Even a champion athlete should select a school on the basis of its academic merits first and its sporting merits second. Don't let a fancy stadium coax you into accepting a school with lousy classes. Your sport is important to you, but the lessons you'll learn in college will stay with you for a lifetime. Make sure they're the right ones.

CHAPTER 25

ENGAGE A CAMPUS VISIT

There are usually three parts of a campus visit. Get the most out of each one.

Visits typically begin with a group information session — someone from the admissions office giving a presentation to a roomful of students and parents. There may be a Q&A at the end. You're not being evaluated at this point — you're doing the evaluating. Do you like what you hear? Is the presenter talking about the things you feel are important? Are there any deal-breakers? Don't be afraid to ask questions. The more information you have, the better-informed your decision will be.

Some campus visits also involve a one-on-one personal interview. This is your chance to tell an admissions representative about yourself. Many medium-sized or highly selective schools conduct these interviews informally, off-campus, as a way to get to know a student, the community, or the schools in the area. Your job at this stage is to make a good impression. Dress well (that means business casual). Sit up straight. Speak up. Provide details. Ask questions.

Then there's the campus tour, usually a walk-around led by a current student. Your job here is to make sure you see everything you came to see. If the guide can't take you to, say, an athletic field, a biology classroom, or a dorm room, ask for directions and plan to visit that place before you leave. The more questions you ask, the better off you'll be. Remember, your guide spends his or her days at this school. Ask what the classes are like, how life is in the dorms, what the food is like, whether the campus has an all-night social life or rolls up the sidewalks at nine p.m. Write out your questions in advance, and add to the list as ideas occur to you — especially any good questions you hear from another student or family.

Don't judge a school by how well the tour guide walks backward. You're in this for an education, not a show.

Finally — and this is the real secret of campus visits — make time to investigate on your own. Visit the classes, the library, the dorms. Imagine yourself there. Is it where you want to be?

CHAPTER 26
GET TO KNOW CURRENT STUDENTS

Once you've done your homework and taken the campus tour, it's time to go off the script. You don't want to know whether this school is a good fit for four out of ten prospective students — you want to know whether it's a good fit for you. And the only way to find that out is to experience college life for yourself.

If you're visiting while classes are in session, arrange to sit in on a class in a subject that interests you. Call or email a professor to set up a one-on-one meeting. Walk around the classrooms and offices in the department where you might be studying. Sit in the library. You'll be spending a lot of time in these places, so it's worth a couple of hours to see what they're like.

Don't confine yourself to academics, either. If you can, arrange an overnight stay in a dormitory to see what student life is like. Eat a meal in the dining hall. Stroll around the campus unsupervised and see what's going on. If nothing else, you'll get a glimpse of the local weather and find out what the students do in their downtime.

Speaking of students, talk to them! Buy him or her lunch. Ask someone why him/her chose this school, and what kind of person does well there. See if you enjoy the community. You may come away with answers to questions you didn't even think to ask.

CHAPTER 27
USE CURRENT STUDENTS

If you wanted to learn about life in a foreign country, you'd ask someone from that country. If you want to learn about life on a college campus, ask a college student.

Most college campuses are pretty friendly places, and most college students who aren't too busy are willing to talk to prospective students. Find an occupied table in the dining hall and introduce yourself. Walk up to someone sitting under a tree in the quad and make friends. Be positive, earnest, and polite. Explain that you're visiting the campus, and maybe break the ice with a joke about trying to find your way around. (Most college campuses are laid out like the nests of squirrels with ADHD. Outsiders get lost easily, the students know it, and it's easy to get a laugh that way.) Ask your new acquaintance if they've got a minute to answer a couple of questions. If the answer is "No," thank them politely and move on. But unless you're touring during final exams, it shouldn't take too long to find a willing informant.

If you can't visit a campus in person, contact the school's alumni association and ask to meet with an alumnus in your area. Find out whether anyone from your high school, your hometown, or your religious organization has attended. Call them up and ask to meet them for coffee. (Offer to buy the coffee if you can — it shows initiative, and people are more likely to say "yes" when free food is involved.) Ask your questions politely, and thank them for their time. You'll be surprised at what you can learn.

THE SCIENCE OF GETTING INTO COLLEGE

CHAPTER 28

INTERVIEW HELL

At most colleges, the interview plays a minor role in the selection process. Its real purpose is to confirm the nice things people said about you in your letter(s) of recommendation and make sure you're not secretly a chainsaw murderer. Most colleges see the interview as an exchange of information — they get to know you personally, and you get to learn firsthand about the school. So really, you're interviewing them while they're interviewing you.

On-campus interviews are usually conducted by admissions officers, or sometimes graduate students or seniors. They're a bit more formal, so dress nicely if you can, sit up straight, and be on your best behavior. Make sure you have questions to ask once the interviewer's finished asking you questions, and review your information about the college ahead of time so you don't get stuck asking obvious ones. Don't be afraid to ask unusual or off-the-wall questions, either; the worst that can happen is someone saying, "I don't know."

Some very selective schools (we call them Tier 1) conduct interviews off-campus. These interviews are less formal, and they're usually conducted by an alumnus. The same rules apply — clean yourself up, present yourself well, and ask your best questions. Don't worry that they'll think you're trying too hard. They know you're nervous and curious, because they are too.

Remember: both parties in the interview have the power to say no. They don't have to admit you, and you don't have to attend. Your job in the interview is to come across as someone genuine, a good fit for the school. Their job is to come across as a place you'll want to go.

CHAPTER 29

ASK THE COLLEGE QUESTIONS

If "know thyself" is the first rule of choosing a college, "know thy schools" is the second. You should develop your own list of things you want to know, but here are some good places to start asking questions of your tour guide or dining-hall expert:

— Who teaches the introductory-level courses? Professors of all ranks? Graduate students?

— How big were your freshman classes? How big are they now?

— Where do students go to socialize?

— What do you do for fun on campus? Off campus?

— What are some of the popular academic departments?

— What other colleges did you apply to? Why did you pick them? Why did you finally choose this one?

— What do you think of the library, residence halls, social life, food, etc.?

— If you could change three features about this college, what would you change?

— What are the big issues (campus-wide, regionally, nationally) that are important to students this year?

— How many students transfer to other colleges or leave the university? Why?

— Is the student body integrated across race, class, major/division, athletes/non-athletes, etc.? Basically, do cliques divide the school or do students mingle with one another?

— How effective is the faculty advising system?

— How do professors relate to students? Are they accessible?

— What academic assistance programs are available for students? (For example, is there a writing center, tutoring, untimed testing, etc.?)

— How accessible, and how capable, is the career services/graduate placement office?

— Which departments are considered outstanding? Which are considered average?

— How much credit do students get for advanced courses in high school — e.g., Advanced Placement exams?

— What opportunities exist for independent study or honors programs? Are students required to write a senior thesis? Are internships available or required?

— What is the student-faculty ratio? Does that statistic include only teaching faculty or all employees?

— What is the average class size? What is the range of class sizes?

— Are most courses cut-and-dry schedules of lectures, exams, a couple of papers and a final? Are there exceptions? What are they like?

— What housing options are available? Can students choose their roommates? Is off-campus housing available, and is it popular?

— If the school has fraternities and sororities, what percentage of the student body lives off-campus? What are the social opportunities (dances, parties, intramural athletics) if you don't join a Greek organization?

— What activities (dances, concerts, speakers, etc.) does the college sponsor? How often? Do most students remain on campus on weekends?

— What types of students are found in the student body? Does any one group dominate the campus atmosphere? What is the national, regional, and local representation? Most popular majors? What percentage of each freshman class graduates in four years? What percentage goes on to graduate training?

— What role do students play in the college's political, social, and academic life? Do they sit on judicial committees or help set policies at any level?

— Are special-interest services available? What types? Are all religious and ethnic groups adequately represented in each class? Are religious facilities available? If the school is church-related, how much emphasis is there on that religion? Is there an Office of Minority Student Affairs, or organizations sponsored by African American, Hispanic, Asian, Native American, or gay and lesbian students? Does the administration support diversity on campus?

— Does the college offer services to help students get on-campus or summer jobs? Is there a Career Planning Office to help students investigate professional options and plan for the future?

— What is the ratio of men to women? If it's a single-sex school, what are the plans for the future? Will the school continue to support single-sex education?

None of these questions has a single "right" answer, but together they're a good way of singling out the school that is right for you.

GETTING IN: MICHAEL

Michael came to me as a senior, after working with a previous counselor. He'd applied to plenty of schools and had been accepted to more than half. But with a 3.65 GPA and a 1950 on the SAT, he felt he could do better. He wanted to get into the Ivy League. Could I help?

I could … so I told him to hit the gym.

Michael was 70 pounds overweight, and I told him that if he was going to spend a year at community college and then try for the Ivy League, he had to get himself straightened out. And he also had to get straight A's —something he'd never done in his life.

Michael accepted my challenge. This kid was at my house every morning to run on the treadmill, use the exercise bike, and swim laps in the pool. He watched his diet and lost 50 pounds in his first six months — and he made straight A's in all 16 units. English, pre-calculus, economics. He got help from his teachers and hired a tutor. He took 18 units that second semester and wrote a fantastic application essay about what it was like to completely change his life. The schools demanded in-progress grade reports, recommendations from his professors. They weren't sold on this miraculous transformation.

Michael sent it all in. He got into every single one of those schools. And all it took was a year in the gym.

CHAPTER 30

DISCOVERING WHAT YOU DON'T WANT
CLARIFIES WHAT YOU DO WANT

If you visit your supposed dream school and find out that it's more of a nightmare — a miserable social environment, terrible classes, hordes of zombies roaming the campus — be delighted.

Why? Because you've found out now. Not when you move into the dorms, not when your first midterms hit, not when you've been in college for a year or two, trying to convince yourself that everything is okay. If the college you thought was perfect isn't the right place for you, it's better to find out before you commit to going there. You'll save yourself a lot of time, a lot of heartache, and a lot of tuition money.

I say it again: it's good to be unhappy.

Visiting a college campus and realizing you'll be unhappy there frees you up to investigate your other options. It puts you one step closer to finding the right school.

As Sherlock Holmes often said, "Once you have eliminated the impossible, whatever remains, however improbable, must be the truth." If you can cross a school off your list, you've eliminated a little bit of the impossible.

So if you're unhappy — smile!

CHAPTER 31

CHOOSING A COLLEGE — DO'S AND DON'TS

DO ...

DON'T ...

Consider all available resources. Look at every school that might interest you, and every way to get to and from there.

Choose a school solely because your friends are going there, or because your relatives have attended a particular school. You're going to college for you, not them.

Think long and hard about what you want college life to be. It's your life, and your goals. The social part of school is the most important factor; <u>the place where you fit in is the place where you'll succeed.</u>

Choose solely based on what you read in a guidebook or on an internet message board. What works for a thousand book buyers may be wrong for you. And since when do you believe everything you read online?

Choose those schools that are within your family's budget and best fit your personal needs. Can you afford it? Is it good for you? Those should be your priorities.

Choose based on the school's national rank or reputation. You are a person, not a statistical approximation. What's right for you is right for you, no matter what U.S. News and World Report says.

Be honest with yourself. In the long run, you'll be happiest if you apply to schools where you honestly feel you will be comfortable academically and socially.

Choose based on how expensive or inexpensive a college is before thoroughly investigating available financial aid. College is expensive. It's why colleges have financial-aid offices. What matters is whether this college is right for you.

Make a decision based on all the information at your disposal. Don't ignore facts because they're inconvenient or uncomfortable — and don't ignore your instincts just because they're not facts. Go with your brain and your gut.

Make a decision based on a good or bad experience that you had during a campus visit or with a tour guide. That's one day of your life, and one person. You wouldn't buy a car based on a 30-second test drive; why would you choose a college based on such a tiny sliver of information?

Do your own independent research. You're the one who will be going to this school. Don't rely on the opinions of others — find out for yourself whether a school will suit you.

Listen to friends and family just because they're your friends and family. It's better to get a great education and have a few lousy Thanksgiving dinners than the other way around.

Keep your top choices to yourself. Where you go to college is your business long before it's anyone else's, and blabbing the names of your dream schools can cause a lot of trouble. If you tell everyone you're applying to Harvard, you risk ruining a few relationships (either because your friends don't have a chance at Harvard or because someone in your circle went to Yale). And if you don't get in, you'll be horribly embarrassed.

Compete with the other candidates in your class and neighborhood. No school can admit every applicant. When the acceptances go out, there will be at least a few hurt feelings and dashed hopes. There's no need to burn your bridges by bragging about all your qualifications, or all your acceptances. You'll only go to one school anyway — and good friendships will last longer than four years.

PART IV:
THE APPLICATION PROCESS

Rick's book answered a thousand hard questions with 50 easy to grasp answers.

— Alexis Koenig

CHAPTER 32
WORK THE STEPS

4-6-2. The college application process breaks down into a few major steps.

First, select the colleges you'll be applying to. It's a good idea to select eight to twelve schools — four "guaranteed" schools where you're 90% sure you'll get in easily with your qualifications, six "reach" schools where you meet some but not all of the admission requirements (think 70% sure), and two "stretch" schools where you're not the ideal candidate but hope springs eternal. Make a list of what each school requires in the way of application paperwork and deadlines.

SCHOOLS. Here's an important tip — make sure at least two of your "safety" schools have rolling admissions (for example, the University of Arizona, the University of Iowa, and Louisiana State). These schools will admit you within four to six weeks after you submit your application, which will take a lot of the pressure off. Add them to your list.

ONLINE ACCOUNT. Next, create accounts on the websites of your various schools. At least one or two will probably use the Common Application (a shared online application used by a lot of schools), so create an account there any time after July 1 of your twelfth-grade year — the earlier, the better. If you're applying to the University of California system (for schools like UCLA and UC Berkeley), create an account any time after September 1 of that year. For all other schools, create an account as soon as you're eligible. Make sure your username and password are something you'll remember.

TRANSCRIPTS & SCORES. Next, gather your resources: an unofficial transcript from your high school(s), your SAT/ACT and SAT-2 test results, your activity log and a list of your senior classes. Check over the applications to see if you need letters of recommendation — and if so, how many and from whom. Get those requests in as early as possible; most of the people you'll want to recommend you will be busy folks. Ask nicely.

REQUIREMENTS. Finally, take an inventory of what each application requires you to do. Look at the essay and short-answer questions. Can you use the same essay for two or more schools? Do you need to write any supplements or personal statements? Begin planning what you'll say.

INSTRUCTIONS. Input the basic information on each application first — your name, your address, and so on. Remember how your elementary-school teachers complained when you didn't write your name on your paper? Now isn't the time to repeat that mistake.

FEES. Fill out your forms, write your essays and short answers (draft and draft and draft again), enclose your checks (keep a Visa or MasterCard available in case a school won't take a check), make copies of all of it, and submit your applications at least one week before the application deadline(s), by one-day or certified mail. I can't stress this enough. So many students apply to these schools that they're always swamped. The earlier you can send in your application, the better, and having a receipt and copies of everything will help you if your paperwork gets mislaid. Make sure you've got a notification email from each school, time- and date-stamped.

SCHOOL COUNSELOR (NAVIANCE). Make certain your test scores, transcripts, and recommendations have been sent on time, too; be sure your school or counselor has a list of your schools with addresses so they can send your transcripts and secondary reports. If your school is using Naviance (a software package that lets high schools keep track of students' applications to make sure records and transcripts have been sent), make sure that all of your colleges are listed in the system and that your Common Application is linked to your Naviance profile. Ask your teachers for letters of recommendation so you can post their names, their email addresses and the subjects they teach in Naviance for colleges to see.

OFFICIAL SCORE. Log into your College Board or ACT account and have your official scores sent to all your colleges. Some schools want to see every score; some want to see the best from each sitting (this is called the superscore). If you're submitting your ACT scores, submit your best sitting. A few schools now superscore your ACT and take your best score from multiple sittings, but unlike the SAT, which displays all your scores on one screen, the ACT lists different sittings separately, so those scores must be ordered independently — and that will cost you each time.

If you're applying to <u>Tier I schools that request subject-test scores and you're using your SAT or ACT scores, you will have to go onto the College Board website and send just your subject-test scores.</u> If you're submitting SAT scores in lieu of ACT scores, then you'll have the option of selecting your best subject-test scores to send.

Do not forget to pay your application fees. Every year, a lot of students submit their applications and supplements and forget the money. Remember — college is a business! Don't screw up your chances by forgetting to pay.

Two weeks after you send your admissions materials, start calling your schools to make sure your file is complete. Too often the College Board, the school registrar, or the teachers filling out your recommendations are all slow in getting their information to your colleges. If you call often, you can make sure nothing falls through the cracks.

If you miss the application deadline (this is very bad news — don't do it if you can avoid it), your only hope is to call the school's Dean of Admission and ask for a waiver of the date. It helps if you have a significant reason for missing it, like a volcano erupting in your backyard, but if you don't have anything that good, beg. And pray.

CHAPTER 33

KISS UP TO YOUR TEACHERS

All your life, you've been told to be your own person. Maintain your dignity. Don't let other people dictate who you are and what you do. Don't kiss up to people even if you want their approval or their help.

Lies! All of it!

If you need letters of recommendation, or even a little help bumping that grade up from a plus to a minus, your first job is to kiss up to your teachers. It's not that your teachers are all petty, vain tyrants who like sycophantic suck-ups — although some of them probably are — but that they see so many kids every day that it's hard to remember anything specific about anyone. They have enough trouble remembering names, let alone personal details.

But they do remember a few students — usually the bright ones who tried extra hard, the kind ones who cared about everyone, and the troublemakers who set their desks on fire. Teachers will remember those kids forever, and if you're in the first or second category, you can get everything you need.

So suck up. Raise your hand to answer questions. Stay after class to clean up and get to know them. Think of good questions to ask the teacher and ask them one-on-one. Ask about their interests. Say "hello" on the way in and "goodbye" on the way out. Stop them in the halls and compliment them on their lessons. Be helpful, be interested, be sincere, and above all be there.

The ultimate dirty trick is forging a relationship with the teacher nobody likes. The grumpy one, the strict one, the very old or very young one — that's the best one for you to get to know. That teacher is looking for a friend. Be his or her only friend, and you'll go far.

When you ask for that recommendation from a teacher who's already on your side, you'll often get a "Yes" before you can finish your sentence.

CHAPTER 34
FOLLOW APPLICATION INSTRUCTIONS

It's tempting to fill your application with everything but the kitchen sink — extra letters of recommendation, a DVD of your violin solo, a testimonial from your kindergarten teacher about your amazing talent for finger-painting. Don't do that.

Many admissions offices don't have the ability or the interest to review materials they didn't ask for. Some of them will even take a fat kitchen-sink application envelope as evidence that you didn't read the instructions on the application forms. And if you didn't follow directions, they can eliminate you right away. Worst of all, too many supplemental materials, especially ones that indicate interests all over the map, can dilute the power of your personal brand, especially if your great achievements turn out to be pretty ordinary in the larger world. (This is why it's important to get an objective evaluation of your talents before you apply.)

These supplements take time and energy to create. Don't waste those resources!

Instead of pimping out your application with spinning rims, limit your extra materials (if you include them at all) to things that support your personal brand and/or compensate for any weaknesses in your profile. If your grades dipped for a year because one of your parents lost a job and you had to work to make ends meet, a letter from your boss describing your work ethic can help explain the gap. If your transcripts don't show your potential as an artist, a letter from a mentor or a sample of a masterpiece can burnish your credentials.

Above all, leave the kitchen sink in the kitchen. Bring only the best to the table.

CHAPTER 35

HOW WILL YOU STAND OUT

When you're trying to present your best possible self, don't sell yourself short. Even if your list of achievements isn't long, play up the ones that show sincere dedication.

Mention things that help you stand out from other students. If you have a passion for chess, the tuba, skiing, basket weaving, computers, Sherlock Holmes, macramé, ballet, photography, classical music, astronomy, cooking, Druids, hobbits, or rock collecting — tell your colleges! Describe your level of talent, the depth of your involvement, and what interesting insights and talents you might bring to a college as a result.

Make sure that your bragging supports your brand, and that your bragging is proportionate. Don't let your most important talents, awards, and activities sink under the weight of a list of everything you've ever won or done. List the most significant and most interesting things about you. Are you a cosplayer who won first prize in a convention masquerade? The bassist in a Celtic K-pop garage band? An Eagle Scout? A foster parent for orphaned kittens? That's what will make you stand out.

Remember, colleges are looking for a certain mix of students — geographically, ethnically, gender-wise, you name it. It's like they're assembling a jigsaw puzzle, one where they begin with the borders and then fill in the middle however they can. They need so many kids from Wyoming, so many from Maine, 50% girls and 50% boys, a good mix of black, white, brown, green, and polka-dotted — you get the idea. After that, the brand comes into play. The ones who stand out are the ones who get in. Are you going to get involved in student government? Run a charitable foundation from your dorm room? Be a star on the football team or in the Shakespeare festival? Whatever you do, do it loud and proud, and lead. They're always looking for leaders.

And if the application asks whether you'll keep up with this interest in college, and there's even a slim chance you might, check yes. And brag some more.

CHAPTER 36
ANSWER THE QUESTIONS

There's an old joke that says you should never ask a lawyer, "Do you have the time?" Any normal person would look at his or her watch and say, "It's 2:15." A lawyer, being a literal-minded so-and-so, will simply look at that watch and say, "Yes."

When writing your personal statement or your essays, write like a lawyer's wristwatch. Look carefully at the question (or questions) you're being asked, and answer exactly. Don't go off on your favorite tangent. Don't try to shoehorn in your favorite funny or inspirational story. Don't let yourself stray too far afield. Answer the question you've been asked. If you've got examples or anecdotes to back up your point, feel free to go crazy — but answer the question you've been asked.

Admissions officers seem to like essays about overcoming adversity, lessons learned from life or from literature, insight into an uncommon experience or achievement, or information about an unusual hobby or interest. You might be asked to write about your personal hero, or an issue that concerns you. Whatever it is, keep the prompt handy while you write, and stick to the word limit. Answering the question is job one.

Do you have the time? Yes, you do.

CHAPTER 37

USE YOUR VOICE

Never underestimate the power of your own voice.

Think about the best book you've ever read, the one you loved most. Can you quote any lines from it? Was there one character who really came alive to you? Did the author's words have their own rhythm, their own sound and feel? Can you hear some of those words even now?

Authors spend years developing that effect. They call it voice, and it means the way they put words and ideas together. Done right, an author's voice becomes a real voice in your head. Professional writers must create hundreds or thousands of original voices for the different things they write. It's the hardest part of the job.

Guess what? You have at least one original voice built in — yours.

Your application essay must be your own words. It's a good idea to get your academic dean or English teacher (or your parents) to review your drafts, but your writing should be your words first and last. <u>Colleges will pay more attention to how you write than to what you write, and the you part is just as important as the how, so write in your own voice.</u> What do you really think? How would you describe an experience? What word would you use for that idea?

When in doubt, write what sounds best, most natural, most true to you. That's your voice. And it's the best tool you have.

CHAPTER 38
YOU HAVE SOMETHING TO WRITE ABOUT

Most application essay prompts boil down to one question: <u>What happened in your life to make you the person you are today?</u>

Maybe you didn't swim from Cuba to the United States to find a better life. Maybe you've never climbed Mount Everest, or mined an asteroid. Maybe you've never led a revolution, or an orchestra, or a Save the Dodo club. But if you've lived this long, you've done or experienced something. And that's your secret weapon.

If you've lived your whole life in the suburbs, behind white picket fences, you might think you have nothing to write about. You're wrong. Think about the best, or worst, day of your life. Think about the person, or the words, that changed everything for you. Think about the thing you never thought you'd do. It can be big or small, mighty or miniscule. What's important is that it matters to you.

I know a student who got into Harvard with an essay about learning to walk. Almost every applicant to Harvard can walk — but for her, walking was a life-changing event. Her essay made it an epic one. If it matters to you, you can make it as dramatic as it needs to be. Start with the wildest, craziest first sentence you can think of. Be creative, be thorough, and grab the reader's attention. Most of all, write from the heart.

Your secret weapon is the fact that only you have lived your life. No one else can write about you. That's all the advantage you need.

CHAPTER 39
BE WILLING TO SHED A TIER

Everybody thinks they want to get into Harvard. Almost everybody is wrong.

Many students think that a big-name, top-of-the-line school like Harvard or Stanford or MIT is the only place to get a real, high-value, "good" education. And these highly competitive schools do a great job. But they're not the only colleges in the world, and they might be the wrong colleges for you.

Harvard and its pals are what we in the business call Tier I schools. They're famous for their rigorous curriculum, overachieving students, and highly competitive admissions process. They're also extremely expensive pressure cookers, with sky-high tuition bills and stressed-out students who are driven to succeed in part because, well, they're at Harvard.

Getting into a Tier I school requires excellent grades and test scores, a high class rank, and a selection of achievements in the right extracurricular activities for your intended major. If these schools need a tiebreaker, they look at SAT-2 subject scores, personal statements, and letters of recommendation. Tier I schools aren't all about who you know, but connections can be important.

Tier II and Tier III schools — that's just about every school you've ever heard of that isn't in Harvard's weight class — are different. They look at your grades and the curriculum of your high school. Their criteria are rigorous high-school curriculum, your personal brand, your class rank, your GPA, and your SAT or ACT scores. The tiebreakers are your subject tests, your personal recommendations and your seventh-semester grades. That's right; if your GPA isn't all it should be, you can swing admission into a Tier II or Tier III school by raising your grades at the eleventh hour.

The advantage to Tier II and Tier III schools for most students is that they're more affordable and less high-stress. Students at lower-tier schools still get an excellent education, but they're more likely to have balanced social lives too, with better physical and emotional health, even years after graduation.

How do I know this? I surveyed 10,000 alumni of my program, The Key. I contacted them when they'd been out of college for one year, three years, five years, and ten years to see how they were doing. At first, the Tier I alumni were doing best — higher pay, better positions, and a laser-like focus on making more money and climbing the ladder as fast as they could. The Tier II and Tier III students were content with their lives — they were mostly managers, salespeople, and graduate students — but wished they'd worked harder in high school and attended a Tier I school.

But at the five-year mark, something changed. The Tier II and Tier III students started moving up. They reached management and executive positions, and reported that they had strong incomes and were happy with their lives. The Tier I alumni were financially successful, too, but had begun to question whether they were in the right job or climbing fast enough. They were less happy than their lower-tier counterparts, who were still doing fine.

Unfortunately, many high-achieving students don't even look at Tier II and Tier III schools because they think that only Tier I will do. They miss out on the smaller classes, more diverse student bodies, and richer campus life that these lesser-known schools can offer. They never realize that they'd be happier, and have more chances to excel, in a slightly more out-of-the-way place.

So if your dream-school list begins and ends with MIT, throw a few lesser-known public and private schools into the mix. Tour their campuses. Sit in on their classes. You might just find the school you didn't even know you were looking for.

GETTING IN: ELENA

On the surface, Elena had it all — an affluent upbringing, a prestigious private high school, decent grades and a few friends. But teenage girls can be cruel, and Elena soon found herself an outcast at school. By junior year, she was seriously depressed.

I set Elena up with volunteer work, tutoring at-risk girls in the inner city. I thought she'd bounce back once she realized what a difference she was making.

I was wrong.

As I watched, Elena pulled deeper and deeper into her shell. She began smoking marijuana and hanging around with dangerous new friends — an older, rougher crowd. Then the marks appeared on her arms. Red, angry welts and cuts. She covered them up, but she couldn't cover everything.

Elena's busy parents didn't have a clue; she wore long sleeves around them, and when her cutting got out of control she'd check into hospitals and then flee when asked for identification, so nobody ever called an adult. As long as Elena's grades stayed high, her parents had no clue that she was locking herself in a room after school every day and taking a razor blade to her skin. Nobody knew how miserable she was — at least, until we finally asked.

After a long string of failed interventions, we ended up bundling her out of the house at 4:30 in the morning and taking her to a wilderness rehab center for nine weeks. Far away from the people who'd supplied her with drugs and encouraged her to cut, she managed to clear her mind and figure out who she really was underneath. <u>She discovered a generous heart, a sharp mind — and a desire to go to college after all. But she was sure that goal was out of reach.</u>

She was wrong.

It took work, but it happened for her. A couple of years, a boatload of counseling, and a lot of clean drug tests later, Elena is finally in college — a school that even her once-oblivious parents agree is a pretty good one, and a great fit for her. She's studying counseling, hoping to help other girls before they find themselves where she did.

And you know what? All those scars are finally beginning to fade …

CHAPTER 40

EARLY DECISION

Early Action and Early Decision programs are great ways to jumpstart your college selection process.

Early Action means applying to a school by November 1. You'll need your test scores, resumé, recommendations, and grades already in order, without any need to take more tests or have a strong seventh semester to make yourself a good candidate. If you've got all that in order, and you have a strong passion to attend a particular school, early application is the way to go. Your chance of acceptance goes up 50% if you apply early, and you can apply to multiple schools with Early Action. It's best to go this route if you're a slam-dunk acceptance — a long shot who applies with the sure-thing Early Action crowd is likely to be deferred or denied.

With Early Action, the school will tell you its decision between December 15 and January 15. If you're accepted, you have the right to make a final decision, which gives you the opportunity to apply to other schools if you want to and make a call by May 1, after the other schools have gotten back to you.

Early Decision is different. The application's still due on November 1, and the school has to decide by December 15, but if you're accepted to an Early Decision school, you must attend it. You're committed. You've accepted a slot there, if one opens up, just by applying. If you're accepted, you must immediately call all the other schools you've applied to and revoke your request for admission.

There's also a sort of middle ground now, called Restricted Early Action. It's relatively new and in place now at Harvard, Stanford, Princeton, Yale, Boston College and Georgetown University. Like Early Decision, Restricted Early Action is a one-school-only deal — no Early Decision elsewhere, and no Early Action elsewhere either. However, if you're accepted under Restricted Early Action, you're not locked in; you can still apply to other schools via regular admission and decide between April and May where you want to attend.

If you know you want to go to a certain school and you've got the qualifications, Early Action and Early Decision are terrific. You do have to prepare earlier — plan out your tests and your application process so that everything's in order by the end of the summer, including your essays. Then you've got the fall to get those recommendations collected, and your best shot at getting into your dream school. And if you get in, the pressure is off. You know where you're going. But with Early Decision, you've got to be sure.

Can you apply to both Early Action and Early Decision? Yes! But your Early Decision school had better be your first choice, because you're locked into going there if a slot opens up, and you can only apply to one Early Decision school no matter how many Early Action schools hear from you.

Choose early, choose often — but choose.

CHAPTER 41

HITCH UP YOUR SAFETY NET

Most public universities and many Tier III private universities offer rolling admission — the chance to apply early in your senior year and, if you meet the school's academic requirements, be accepted within four to six weeks, before most early applicants have even sent their materials in. For example, the University of Arizona automatically admits students with a GPA of 3.1 or higher, a 1650 SAT, and/or membership in the top 25% of their classes — make two out of those three, and you're in.

Make one out of three, however, and you are conditionally admitted. That means the college can request another set of test scores, seventh-semester grades, extra recommendations, and so on. If you meet those criteria, your admission is contingent on successful academic completion of high school. If you keep up the good work, you're in. If your performance deteriorates, the school can revoke its offer of admission.

I can't say this enough: rolling admission is a good thing. Apply to at least two schools that have it. Being accepted to at least one school early in your senior year takes a lot of pressure off you and your family. It might not be your school of choice, but it's a good safety net.

PART V:
WHAT HAPPENS NEXT

I thought grades and test scores were all that was required. I just did not get how much more was needed or how much more the other admissions criteria meant. Getting In is worth every penny.
                                                    – Carl Conrad

CHAPTER 42
A SMALL ENVELOPE COULD BE ACCEPTANCE

In the old days, colleges would send out two kinds of correspondence to applicants. Big packages were acceptances — oversized envelopes stuffed with catalogs and instructions on how to register for classes and campus housing, and maybe a glossy magazine or a hefty acceptance certificate. Then there were small letters — thin, flimsy business-size envelopes with only a sheet or two inside. You still get these letters. These are rejections, according to conventional wisdom, and there's no need to even open them.

Conventional wisdom is wrong. Wrong, wrong, wrong, wrong, wrong! Open that small envelope! Open it as soon as it arrives!

The fact is, many colleges now send out acceptances in those small envelopes. Those glossy extras are expensive, so a lot of students get a short letter of acceptance, or an email, with links leading them to information on housing, student life, timelines, and registration. Large packages, if they're sent, are expensive to mail, so they often travel more slowly, which means the acceptance letter may get to you first even if the acceptance and package are mailed on the same day. What if your dream school accepts you with a small envelope and you never open it because you're afraid of bad news?

A small acceptance means there's probably an email somewhere, maybe stuck in your spam filter. Don't assume that small envelope is a rejection just because it's small. Good things come in small packages. Open it!

CHAPTER 43

SAY "YES" TO THE BEST

If your first-choice school accepts you, say yes.

This may seem obvious. Of course you're going to say yes; it's your first choice. But what if you can't decide? What if you're not sure? What if you wake up in a cold sweat every night, convinced you're making a horrible mistake?

If you're lucky enough to be accepted to more than one school and can't make up your mind, visit the campuses again. Visit the offices of your potential major, and get the name of a good professor. Show up to his or her class 10 to 15 minutes early, get permission to sit in, and soak up the energy. See if it feels right.

You don't have a lot of time; most schools accept their new classes between March 1 and April 15, and require an answer (with a deposit for housing and possible tuition) by May 1. So go over your information again. Walk the grounds. Eat in the commons. Hit the gym. Walk the neighborhood like a student; go to the local grocery store and check out the off-campus housing. Drive a two-mile radius around the school and see what's there.

If you really can't make up your mind, you can usually put down deposits at multiple schools, but this should be a last resort. You'll lose that deposit on any school you decide not to attend, and by taking up a freshman spot you won't use, you will be withholding an opportunity from some other student who really wants to attend that school. So make a decision, and stick with it.

Think long and hard — and then decide. Say yes to the best.

CHAPTER 44
MAKE ANOTHER CAMPUS VISIT BEFORE YOU ACCEPT

Congratulations! You've been accepted! Now go make one last campus visit!

Spend a night in the dorms. Eat in the cafeteria. Hit the campus gym. Spend a day or two living the lifestyle to make absolutely sure that you want to attend the school you think is your first choice. Try to make your visit cover at least one weekday of classes, plus at least one weekend day or night; that way you can sample the social life as well as the academic one. If one or more of your friends has been accepted too, it's okay to make the trip as a group, but once you get there, split up and explore the school solo. It's your decision to make, not theirs.

Why should you do this? Well, there's a big difference between walking around a school like it's Disneyland and standing in the quad with the knowledge that you could actually end up there just by signing a form. Something that annoyed you slightly on your first visit could become a deal-breaking problem once you know what your real options are. Something you overlooked last time might move a second- or third-choice school up to first place. There's no substitute for experience.

And if your opinion doesn't change, you can sign that form and move into the dorms in August, secure in the knowledge that this really is the right school for you.

CHAPTER 45

THE LAST SEMESTER OF YOUR SENIOR YEAR

Senioritis kills.

You're in your last semester of high school. You've been accepted to multiple colleges. It's time to relax, right?

Wrong!

Stay focused. Study hard. Don't drop classes. Finish the race strong. All acceptances are conditional — if you blow off your last semester and your grades slip below your college's requirements, the school can always change its decision to admit you. They can revoke their offer. Try explaining that at graduation!

Just as important, your eighth semester is your last semester of high school. <u>Maybe you loved it and maybe you hated it, but you'll never come back. This is the only life you get. You don't want to spoil your memories of these years — whether they're good or bad</u> — with the fact that your last semester sucked because you couldn't be bothered to show up. Graduation will come soon enough; you don't need to spoil the time you have left.

So show up. Work hard. Finish strong. Walk across that stage and accept your diploma with your head held high. You've done great things, and you're going on to greater ones.

CHAPTER 46
PRACTICE WAIT TRAINING

If you've been wait-listed, don't freak out.

A wait list is a list of students who qualify for admission but haven't gotten in. Schools only wait-list students that they want to admit but can't accommodate yet. The school may be able to offer you a spot after May 1, when those students who have been admitted decide whether or not they're actually going. (Remember how you applied to multiple schools? So did they — and some of them will choose a school other than yours.)

Unfortunately, May 1 is still your decision deadline, too. <u>If you've been wait-listed at your dream school and accepted at your next best choice, you have a decision to make.</u> Do you put down a deposit at the safe school, or stake everything on a dream?

Pay the money. It's insurance.

In the meantime, market yourself to your dream school. <u>Do well in your eighth semester. Send the admissions committee updated grades and new letters</u> of recommendation from your teachers, college alumni, or other prominent people. Do whatever it takes to make sure that the admissions team, the president of the university, or anyone who can help gets you into that school. <u>Get your allies calling and writing letters.</u> Make sure you're never far from mind.

If you get in, you're losing that deposit but going to your dream school. If you don't, you're still going to a good college — one that you chose, remember? You win either way. So marshal your forces, get a grip, and wait.

CHAPTER 47

BE YOUR OWN ADVOCATE

An acceptance is not a sure thing. It is always conditional.

Colleges and universities can withdraw their offers of admission if your grades drop in your final semester, or something comes up that makes you an unsuitable candidate. But even if you're un-accepted, you can fight back.

If your grades have slipped, get out in front of the problem. Contact the university to explain your situation. Maybe there are extenuating circumstances — an illness, a family crisis, a natural disaster. Mention those, and take responsibility for anything you might have done to make the situation worse. The more upfront you are about the problem, the less severe its impact will be. Collect extra letters of recommendation and explanation. Pick up extra qualifications if you can — nothing balances an unexpected B in math like winning a prestigious essay contest. Stay in regular contact with college administrators; send them progress reports, so they know you're working on the problem.

Above all, don't lose your cool. Panic only makes a disaster worse. Explain to the college that whatever's wrong is temporary, fixable, and not going to happen again. Your poise and self-assurance will take you far.

And pull those grades up. It can only help. Getting In: Jared

Jared was homeless, and that was probably the least interesting thing about him.

I found out about Jared from his high-school principal. Fantastically intelligent, Jared was mostly self-taught because he'd grown up with one parent missing and one strung out on drugs. From age nine, he lived mostly on the streets of San Francisco, scavenging food off tables at Taco Bell and reading through the public library. Nobody knew he was a genius. Nobody knew he was in so much trouble. Nobody saw Jared at all until that principal looked, and called a college consultant who was used to working with the children of the rich and famous.

There was no way Jared could afford my rates, but once I'd talked to him, I didn't care. I took him on as a client because I knew he belonged at a top-flight school. And once I explained myself, Jared was determined to seize the opportunity.

I worked with Jared for three years. I helped him get a job at Taco Bell so he could earn both money and food, which let him bring his grades up from B's and C's to straight A's. He moved into a foster home with a nice middle-class family I'd known for years, and insisted on paying them part of his wages even as he crammed for the SAT. He finished high school with a 4.0 GPA and more honors courses than I could count on both hands.

With a story like his, colleges fell all over themselves to recruit him. Wouldn't you?

Jared's at UCLA now, headed for law school, and spending his weekends tutoring kids on skid row. When I ask him what he wants to do with his future, he's got some pretty clear ideas about getting into the courtroom and helping the down and out. I pity anyone who stands in his way. Growing up in the United States, most kids hear that they can do anything if they work hard enough. We don't take it seriously. We say it's just a convenient myth.

Then someone like Jared comes along and makes us wonder if we might be wrong ...

CHAPTER 48

CELEBRATE!

You've been accepted to a great school. Your final high-school grades are rock-solid. You know where you're going and how you're getting there. You've followed your star, done your homework, and turned a chicken into an eagle. You are done, baby.

Time to celebrate!

Even if you're the nose-to-the-grindstone type, there comes a time to relax, and this is it. Don't get too crazy, but take a day or two to enjoy the moment. Go to the beach. Watch a movie with your friends. Eat a cookie. Whatever you do to reward yourself, do it. You've earned it, and you will need it.

The mad scramble to get ready for college will start soon. You'll have to register for classes, sign about a billion forms, and pack up your stuff to move. Your whole life will be changing.

But that's tomorrow. Enjoy today. The rest will do you good, recharging your batteries for the great adventure ahead.

And besides, who doesn't like cookies?

CHAPTER 49

PREPARE FOR FRESHMAN YEAR

If you thought getting into college was a lot of work, actually going to college will make your head spin.

You'll have to fill out and sign a truly ridiculous amount of paper — registration forms, housing documents, insurance, and waivers up the yingyang. Be sure to fill it all out and send it in on time. You are now entering the adult world of paperwork; don't start by screwing it up.

If you've lived in one place all your life and will now be moving to student housing, start planning that move as soon as possible. Make lists of what you want to take and what you can leave behind. Remember that everything is heavier than it looks, and that your dorm room is always smaller than you think. Remember too that your roommate will see everything you cart in and have to live with all of it. You can get away with a couple of raggedy childhood stuffed animals, but leave the rest of the menagerie at home.

Speaking of roommates, contact yours as far in advance as possible. Get to know him or her. Hang out together in person if you can, or online if you can't. You'll be spending a lot of time together, so don't go in blind.

Spend time with your friends and family, too. Yes, you've known them all your life, but soon you'll have a different life. Don't leave before you leave. Bake cookies with your mom, kick a ball with your little brother, and go camping with your cousins one last time.

Thank everyone who has helped you on your journey. It's a good idea to write actual paper thank-you notes to people who wrote letters of recommendation, helped you through your classes, and smacked you upside the head when you needed it. Such letters are rare, and will be treasured. You will be glad to be remembered fondly.

Your new life is coming. Get ready.

CHAPTER 50

GETTING INTO COLLEGE: THE TIMELINE

SIXTH GRADE

March – Research summer educational programs or academic camps, public and private.

April – Formalize your summer strategy for enhanced-education camps, workshops, and tutorials.

June – August – Enroll in advanced math (algebra, if possible), English, social science, and a foreign language (if possible).

SEVENTH GRADE

September – Get settled at school. Read one book of your choice per month and write a paragraph describing what you learned. Begin creating your activity sheet—time spent per week and per month on each activity, office held, and awards received.

April – Enroll in next year's classes — advanced math (algebra or geometry if possible), English, social science, science, and foreign language (if possible).

June – August – Read one book of your choice per month and write a three-paragraph essay describing what you've learned. The three paragraphs should include an introductory paragraph, body paragraph, and conclusion paragraph.

EIGHTH GRADE

September – January – Get acclimated to school. Work hard in core courses and engage in school and outside activities.

January – Prepare for private high-school admission.

February – March – Take private-school exams; continue to pursue school and outside interests.

April – Review your scores from private-school exams. Plan summer activities (camps, summer school, community service).

May – June – Visit high schools to get a feel for the surroundings.

June – Graduation. Register for high-school classes.

August – Review available class schedules. Make sure you take no less than five core classes (math, science, English, social science, and foreign language).

FRESHMAN YEAR

September – Get involved with the student population. Get to know your teachers. Join three clubs and try to become an elected officer.

October – Sign up for, and take, the PSAT.

December – Get PSAT scores. Review scores and begin troubleshooting wrong answers.

February – Prepare for the SAT-2 subject tests in Biology, Chemistry, Math 1, and Math 1C. Freshmen taking this test should be in upper-level classes with a mastery of the subject areas outlined. Note: If you're going to take an AP exam in one of these subjects, then it's premature to take the SAT-2 right now.

March – May – Sign up for the SAT-2s (if you're prepared). Decide on summer plans: summer school, college summer programs, talent programs, travel, etc. Register for sophomore classes. Focus on the most rigorous curriculum and at least five core classes: English, history, math, science, and a foreign language.

June – Take the SAT-2s in the first weekend of June. Make sure to participate in summer enhancement or some learning activity.

July – August – Prepare for the PSAT (untimed). Work on vocabulary words, work on strategies for the analogies and sentence completions, work on reading comprehension (timed), and review algebra and geometry.

SOPHOMORE YEAR

August – September – Take at least five core classes. Get to know your teachers, sign up for clubs, focus on leadership roles in clubs and activities, prepare for the PSAT (timed), take practice tests, review wrong answers, and work on vocabulary words.

October – Sign up for the PSAT. Take the PSAT.

December – Get PSAT scores back. Review scores and practice problems.

January – Visit colleges on winter break if time allows.

February – Prepare for the SAT-2 subject tests in Biology, Chemistry, Math 1, and Math 1C. Sophomores taking this test should be in upper-level classes with a mastery of the subject areas outlined. Note: If you're going to take an AP exam in one of these subjects, then it's premature to take the SAT-2 right now.

March – May – Sign up for SAT-2s if prepared. Over spring break, visit colleges. Decide on summer plans: summer school, college summer programs, talent programs, travel, etc.

June – Take the SAT-2s in the first weekend of June. Make sure to participate in summer enhancement or some learning activity.

July – August – Prepare for the PSAT (timed). Work on vocabulary words, work on strategies for the analogies and sentence completions, work on reading comprehension (timed), and review algebra and geometry.

JUNIOR YEAR

August – September – Take at least five core classes. Get to know your teachers, sign up for clubs, focus on leadership roles in clubs and activities, prepare for the PSAT (timed), take practice tests, review wrong answers, and work on vocabulary words.

October – Sign up for the PSAT. Take the PSAT.

December – Get your scores back from the PSAT and review. Troubleshoot answers.

January – Sign up for the March, April, and May SAT. Sign up for the April and June ACT.

Start thinking about what you want in a college. What size school do you want to attend? How far away from home do you want to be? What kind of weather do you want? What social atmosphere do you prefer? Do you want to be in a city, residential area, college town, or a rural environment? Send away for college viewbooks and videos. Plan a spring-break college trip.

February – Prepare for the SAT I (timed). Take a 30-minute section test daily (alternate the verbal sections with the math section). Take full practice tests once a week — Sunday morning is good.

Spring Break – Visit colleges. Decide on summer plans: summer school, college summer programs, talent programs, travel, etc.

April – Visit colleges. Go on tours. Go to information sessions.

May – Take AP exams. (Prepare in school for individual classes.) Take the SAT-1 test. Prepare for the June ACT test; take 35 – 60 minutes daily (alternate sections) and take full timed ACT practice tests on Sunday mornings.

June – Take the SAT-2s. Take the ACT. Begin writing a rough draft of your personal statement, send away for college applications, begin a draft of your resumé, and decide on teacher recommendations.

SENIOR YEAR

July – August – Finalize your academic resumé. Visit schools to narrow down your choices. Go to interviews. Write second and third drafts of your personal statement. Work on short-answer essays. Follow up on applications to schools that interest you. Sign up for the SAT-1, ACT, and SAT-2s for September and October.

September – Review for the SAT-1. Copy college applications and put away the originals until you're ready to type them up. Fill out practice applications, finalize your resumé, apply for scholarships, and work on each school's essay in rough-draft form. Review for the ACT and SAT-2s. Apply to rolling admission at a "sure thing" school. Finalize college applications.

October – Type up secondary-school reports. Get teacher recommendations and complete the first part of your applications. Give your resumé, reports, and recommendations to the appropriate people. Take the SAT-1. Start sending out completed applications. Send those first parts away to schools with checks enclosed. Set up alumni interviews. Finish all early-action or early-decision applications. Apply to rolling admission at a "sure thing" school. Apply for scholarships.

November – Applications are due for the University of California. Take the SAT-1, ACT, and SAT-2 exams if needed. Finish essays for regular-admission applications and type up the final drafts of your applications for regular admissions. Apply for scholarships.

December – Take the ACT, SAT-1, and SAT-2s for the last time. Pick up a free application for Federal Student Aid (FAFSA), pick up a CSS/PROFILE for private schools, and copy and fill out both forms. Receive acceptance from early-action, early-decision, and rolling-admission schools. Hand in your mid-year grade reports to the appropriate registrars.

January – Send your FAFSA and CSS/PROFILE for processing. Apply for scholarships.

February – April – Your acceptances arrive. Make plans for an overnight visit (by yourself!) at your final-choice universities, and make your decision. Send in your housing deposit, accept and refuse admission as appropriate, and negotiate for financial aid.

May – May 1 is your deadline to register for the college you have chosen. Get your deposit and housing requests in, and sign up for college proficiency exams if needed.

June – Graduate. Go on your senior trip. Pack your bags and clean your room. You're going to college!

It is obvious that we can
no more explain a passion
to a person who has never
experienced it than we can
explain light to the blind.
                    – T. S. Eliot

The Key's programs help your son or daughter to identify their strengths, unlock their potential, choose the right college, position themselves for admission, and outline a course of study and extracurricular experiences to lead to a life of success

CONTACT: RICK SINGER
916. 384. 8802
www.thekeyworldwide.com
265 Hartnell Place
Sacramento, CA 95825

If you are reading this testimonial than you understand how overwhelming, intimidating & confusing the college application process is…

As a mother of three, I have heard far too many "professional" and personal opinions on what colleges are looking for in your student. Rick Singer delivers the most straight forward and uncomplicated approach I have heard. I wish that all of my children had the benefit of reading "Getting In" to the college of their choice before they began. The way Singer communicates that whatever your passion is, it is the right one. Just have one. This Is so refreshing. Don't just do something because it will look good on an application. Unfortunately, grades do matter and so does class selection. Singer gives excellent examples of how to help your student push their self and be honest about trying their best. If your student can follow the uncomplicated advice Singer delivers in the pages of his book they will, not only have a more rewarding experience, they will discover what is the right college for them. Not anyone else. Most importantly, they will get into the college of their choice.
— Brigitte C. - Mom

Rick Singer's how-to book: "Getting In" provides both the student and parent, looking to maximize their college admissions opportunities, with the comfort that comes only from having all the information required to make well informed decisions. Knowing exactly what to expect with a what to do plan affords anyone facing this challenging experience with the means to calmly see it through successfully.
— Mike M.

If "Getting In" to college matters, then Rick Singer's book is a must read. Mr. Singer's 50 Secrets both identify and simplify the process and issues every college applicant will face no matter the college he or she identifies as the "perfect" or "only" acceptable school. Give your child the very best chance of being admitted to the college of their choice by reading and following the 50 Secrets Mr. Singer, with almost 30 years of college admissions and life counseling experience, is willing to share.
— Chuck K.

Made in the USA
San Bernardino, CA
16 May 2015